PUFFIN LITTLE

Little Environmentalist

PUFFIN BOOKS

UK | USA | Canada | Ireland | Australia
India | New Zealand | South Africa | China

Penguin
Random House
Australia

Penguin Random House Australia is part of the Penguin Random House group of companies
whose addresses can be found at global.penguinrandomhouse.com.

First published by Puffin Books, an imprint of Penguin Random House Australia Pty Ltd, in 2021

Printed in China

A catalogue record for this
book is available from the
National Library of Australia

NATIONAL
LIBRARY
OF AUSTRALIA

ISBN 978 1 76 104170 9

penguin.com.au

PUFFIN  LITTLE

Gardening

PUFFIN BOOKS

HELLO, LITTLE ENVIRONMENTALISTS WELCOME TO MY GARDEN ...

You've come by at just the right time –
I'm about to water all of my plants!

So grab your hat and sunscreen
and join me in the GARDEN!

Looking
after a
garden can
be a lot of work,
but it's very important.

Plants do so much for our environment. They help to keep our air clean, provide food and homes for local wildlife and they can provide food for us to eat.

Plus they're very pretty to look at!

It's so nice to be outdoors!

As Little Environmentalists, we know that we need to take care of animals *and* plants to have a healthy planet.

So I'm going to tell you all about plants and show you how gardens can really help our environment.

We might be LITTLE, but we've got some **BIG** facts to learn.

Are you ready?

Then turn the page . . .

GARDENS ARE THE PLACES WE GROW PLANTS

There are so many different types of gardens!

They can be as big as a backyard or as small as a single pot on a windowsill.

They can be inside or out, or even on a roof.

They can be planted in the ground, in a collection of pots or perhaps in an assortment of old boots.

They can be full of trees or flowers or plants that can be eaten.

They can be in places that receive lots of sunlight and rain, or only a little.

A garden can be whatever we make it!

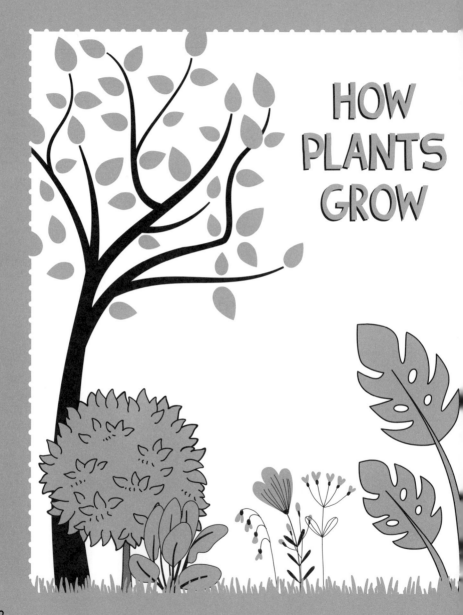

HOW PLANTS GROW

A plant is a living thing that uses sunlight to make its own food.

Along with sunlight, plants also need carbon dioxide and water to survive.

A plant could be a kind of tree, flower, moss, grass, fern, herb, bush or seaweed.

How does sunlight, carbon dioxide and water become food? Well, Little Environmentalists, to find out, we need to learn all about plants and a process called photosynthesis.

WHAT MAKES A PLANT

Before we dive into photosynthesis, let's look at the different parts that make up a plant.

- ◎ **Leaves** collect energy from the sun and turn it into food via photosynthesis.
- ◎ The **stem** is like a spine, helping plants grow tall and strong, and holding the pathways for nutrients and water to travel throughout the plant.
- ◎ **Roots** are the parts of plants that live underground and pull nutrients and water from the soil.

DID YOU KNOW?

Not all plants have leaves, stems and roots?

Some plants, like moss, don't have roots. Other plants, like cacti, don't have leaves.

PHOTOSYNTHESIS

Photosynthesis is the process through which plants turn SUNLIGHT into FOOD.

First, plants absorb and trap energy from the sun. They do this with the help of the special pigment that turns their leaves green, which is called chlorophyll.

Then they mix the sunlight with two other ingredients: water (which plants absorb from the soil) and carbon dioxide (which plants absorb from the air).

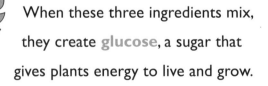

When these three ingredients mix, they create glucose, a sugar that gives plants energy to live and grow.

Ta da! That's photosynthesis!

There's one other thing that is created during photosynthesis. Something that plants don't need, but is essential for almost all other life on earth. Oxygen.

This is good news for us, Little Environmentalists.

Plants remove carbon dioxide from our atmosphere (the air) and replace it with oxygen.
By removing carbon dioxide – one of the greenhouse gases that is changing Earth's climate – plants are helping to keep our atmosphere in balance.

It's one of the most important processes on the planet.

It takes a lot of plants to balance Earth's climate, so it's a good thing that plants are excellent at reproducing. Most new plants grow from seeds.

A seed is made up of a plant embryo, food for the embryo as it grows and a hard protective coating.

Seeds are surrounded by fruit. That's right, Little Environmentalists – the fleshy parts of apples and bananas you enjoy eating has been grown to keep seeds safe. It's also there to encourage animals to eat them!

In the wild, plants rely on animals and birds to help move their seeds to new places.

When an animal eats a fruit, it also eats the seeds. The seeds are then carried around until they make it all the way through the animal's digestive system and return to the ground.

Now the seeds can germinate.

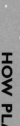

GERMINATION

When a seed gets enough sunlight and water, it starts to sprout. This process is called germination.

Let's watch some seeds grow!

You'll need:

- ◎ a clear glass jar with any old labels removed
- ◎ a few seeds – beans grow very quickly
- ◎ paper towel
- ◎ water

Wet a piece of paper towel, then scrunch it up loosely and place it in the jar. Continue until your jar is full of crumpled, damp paper towel.

Carefully push your seeds down the side of the jar so they sit between the paper towel and the glass.

Place your jar in a bright spot for several days. Make sure to add more water when your paper towels start to dry out!

The first sign of germination you will see is when the seeds split at the sides. Then each seed will sprout a root that will soon be covered in smaller root hairs. Finally, you'll see a stem emerge and leaves will start to grow.

Voilà! You've grown a plant!

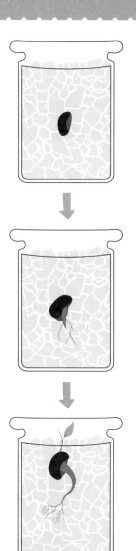

Over 80 per cent of plants on Earth have flowers. Flowers contain pollen, which is carried between plants by pollinators. Once a flower has received the pollen from a matching plant, it can produce seeds.

Without pollinators, we wouldn't have seeds.

Without seeds, most of the plants on our planet wouldn't be able to reproduce, which means that few new plants would grow.

The fewer plants there are, the less likely it is that the Earth can continue to support life.

Wow, plants are super important, aren't they?

POLLINATORS

Pollinators are creatures that carry pollen from one flower to another.

Bees, butterflies, birds, bats and even humans can be pollinators.

Pollen *can* move between plants on the wind and in flowing water, but without the help of pollinators it's a less effective way to travel.

NON-FLOWERING PLANTS

One fifth of all the plants on Earth are non-flowering plants. That's quite a lot!

Big Environmentalists have put them into two groups.

1. PLANTS THAT HAVE SEEDS

Without flowers, non-flowering plants can't produce fruit to protect their seeds. Instead, they use structures called cones to shield their seeds and help them spread. Male cones produce pollen and female cones hold seeds.

Cycads, conifers and ginkgo trees are all non-flowering plants that produce seeds.

2. PLANTS THAT HAVE DUST-LIKE PARTICLES CALLED SPORES

Plants that don't have flowers *or* seeds reproduce with spores. Spores are tiny cells that are carried on the air.

Unlike seeds, they don't need pollen to be able to reproduce. When a spore lands somewhere with the right conditions, it begins to grow into a plant that's exactly the same as the plant it came from.

Mosses, and most ferns and seaweeds, are non-flowering plants that produce spores.

PLANNING YOUR GARDEN

Well, Little Environmentalists, wasn't it exciting to learn all about how plants grow?

Before we can start planting, there
are some important things we need to
consider to make sure our garden grows
as lush and vibrant as it can be.

Are you ready to plan the perfect garden?

UNDERSTANDING YOUR GARDEN

Here are a few of the things that every Little Environmentalist needs to think about when starting a new garden.

IS YOUR GARDEN SUNNY?

One important thing to check is the available light! A windowsill might be in the sun for several hours of the day, or a garden in a walled backyard might be shaded for all but the middle of the day. Don't forget that the available light can vary within very large gardens too!

Check in each hour and note what kind of light your garden receives throughout the day.

ALL ABOUT LIGHT

Plants that need **full sun** require at least six hours of direct sunlight per day.

Plants that need **part sun** or **part shade** require around three hours of direct sunlight per day.

Plants that need **full shade** should get almost no direct sunlight per day.

Indoor plants often require **bright light** or **filtered/indirect light**. Test the light by holding your hand near a clean background, like a wall. Bright light casts a sharp, clear shadow and indirect light a soft one.

29

HOW MUCH SPACE DO YOU HAVE?

Some plants need more space around or above them than others. A vertical garden attached to a wall will likely only be home to short plants, and if you want to plant a tree that will become very large, it's best not to do so right beside a wall, path or driveway.

HOW WILL YOUR PLANTS IMPACT EACH OTHER?

While gardens in pots can be moved around, those in garden beds or planted into the ground can't. So it's important to think about how your plants will interact.

Will any of your plants block out sun for other plants? How tall and wide will each plant grow? Are any of your plants likely to spread rapidly and steal space from others?

WILL YOU BE USING POTS?

Make sure to think about how you'll expand if your plants outgrow their starting pots.

You'll also need to think about what happens when you water your plants. Most plants hate having wet roots, so you'll need to ensure your pots have adequate drainage. Self-watering pots, which hold soil above drained water, are a good option!

For other pots, don't forget to use a saucer to stop excess water spilling on the floor.

MAKING A
RECYCLED POT

As Little Environmentalists, we know that re-using and recycling are very important.

Creating your own recycled pot is as easy as re-using an old container and filling it with potting mix.

Remember to make sure your recycled pot has drainage! Ask a Big Environmentalist to help you drill or bore holes into your container to ensure water can flow out and your plant won't have soggy roots.

Almost anything can be recycled into a pot! Here are some ideas to get you started.

 **Eggshells** make excellent homes for germinating seeds. Put a little soil and a single seed into each shell, and wait for your seedlings to grow.

Old **buckets** can easily become pots once they've had a few drainage holes bored in, and so can **bottles**, **ice-cream containers** and even **gumboots!**

Wheelbarrows and **bathtubs** make excellent planter boxes. Bathtubs even have a drainage hole already built in.

What else could you use as a pot?

PLANNING YOUR GARDEN

It's important to think about your local climate when choosing plants for your garden. The plants that live in the rainforest are very different to plants living in a desert.

This is because different areas have different climates. Knowing your climate can help you choose plants that will thrive in your garden.

TROPICAL climates in northern Australia are hot throughout the year and are usually quite humid, with a distinct wet and dry season.

 SUBTROPICAL climates along Australia's east coast are also quite warm and humid, but they don't usually have wet and dry seasons.

 DESERT climates in central Australia get very little rain and are therefore very dry. This makes it hard for most plant life to grow.

 GRASSLAND climates inland that receive more rainfall than deserts. The temperatures here are less extreme than deserts too.

 TEMPERATE climates on the south and east coasts have warm summers and cool winters, and get enough rain to support most plant life.

LITTLE TOOLS

There are lots of different tools Big Environmentalists use in the garden, but there are only a few you need to get started ...

TOOLS FOR WATERING

Your plants need water to survive! Even outdoor gardens will sometimes need a helping hand.

 **watering can**

 misting bottle

 or even an old jar

TOOLS FOR PLANT CARE

Whether it's repotting an indoor plant, pruning trees and shrubs or turning over fresh mulch in your outdoor garden, these tools should have you sorted.

 **trowel**

 fork

 **secateurs**

GARDENING CLOTHES

Wear these clothes to make sure you're protected from the dirt, water and sun!

gloves   boots

hat

EXTRA BITS AND PIECES

You might find these extra tools useful in the garden too.

plant
labels

dustpan
and brush

rake

compost
bin

UNDERSTANDING YOUR PLANTS

Let's start thinking about plants! When you buy a new plant or a packet of seeds from a garden centre, plant shop or hardware store, there's usually a care label attached.

This label tells you important things you need to know about keeping your new plant happy and healthy.

Your plant label will generally tell you:

- ◎ the name of your plant
- ◎ how much light it needs
- ◎ how big it will grow
- ◎ what kind of soil it prefers
- ◎ how much water it needs
- ◎ and other general care instructions

Now let's put all of this information together, Little Environmentalists. It's time to make some decisions and start **planning your garden!**

- ◎ What plants are you going to choose for your garden?
- ◎ When will you plant them?
- ◎ How much sunlight do they need?
- ◎ How often will you need to water them? What about fertilising and pruning?
- ◎ If they're plants that will have a harvest, when will they be ready to pick?

Hmm, that's a lot to think about. You'll need somewhere to write all of these decisions down . . .

KEEPING A GARDEN JOURNAL

Creating a garden journal is the perfect way to keep everything you need to know all in one place.

Your journal could be an exercise book, a special notebook, on a computer or tablet or even a collection of loose-leaf paper. It can also be as extravagantly decorated or simple as you like!

Use your garden journal to plan your garden; record the names and care information for your plants; and note when you last did things like watering, weeding, fertilising, pruning or repotting your plants.

You can also draw pictures of your plants, note when you last harvested your kitchen garden, paste photos of your garden, record the weather . . . the possibilities are endless!

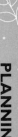

CARING FOR YOUR GARDEN

Now that we've learnt all about how plants grow and planned our garden, let's add some plants!

Caring for a garden is a big responsibility. We're going to learn some LITTLE things that make a BIG difference to the health of our gardens.

Let's get started!

SOIL

Different plants grow best in different kinds of soil. Some plants, such as cacti, prefer sandy soil that can't hold much water, but most plants like rich soil with lots of nutrients in it.

Don't forget to check your plant's label to see which soil will make your plants happiest. There are also lots of different things you can add to your soil to make it perfect for your garden.

One of the best things to add to any soil is compost!

Compost adds rich organic matter to your garden, increases drainage in clay soils or helps sandy soils retain moisture, keeps soil at the right acidity and much more. Plus it means your kitchen scraps are helping to grow even more plants.

Rich, healthy soil is a lovely home for worms and other bugs that turn leaf litter and natural waste into the nutrients our plants need to grow big and strong.

Would you like to learn how to make your own compost?

MAKE YOUR OWN COMPOST

Compost is **easy** to make at home, no matter how big your garden is!

You'll need:

- ◎ a container with holes drilled into it, or a raised, walled enclosure in your garden
- ◎ water
- ◎ a small garden fork
- ◎ greens like vegetable offcuts, old tea bags, bread, eggshells, grass clippings or plant trimmings
- ◎ browns like leaf litter, shredded cardboard and paper, straw, woodchips or twigs

Place your container in a dry, partly shaded spot.

Prepare your greens and browns by asking a Big Environmentalist to help you chop them into pieces. This will help them become compost faster!

Place a thin layer of browns at the bottom of your container, followed by a layer of greens. Continue until your container is nearly full, but you still have enough space to be able to mix up your compost.

Add a small amount of water to your container so your layers are moist, but not wet.

Check on your compost every week or so. Add more water if necessary, more greens and browns if you have them and give it all a mix with your garden fork. After a couple of months you'll have lovely, nutrient-rich soil.

But why do plants need nutrients?

NUTRIENTS

Well, we learnt that plants create glucose, a type of sugar, through photosynthesis. But just like you and me, plants can't survive on sugar alone.

There are three main nutrients that plants need:

- ◎ **nitrogen** for healthy green leaves
- ◎ **phosphorous** for tough roots and for making flowers, fruits and seeds
- ◎ **potassium** for strong stems and speedy growth

Worms already give a big nutrient boost to in-ground gardens, but balcony and indoor gardens can benefit from these wriggly critters too . . . with a worm farm!

Worm farms are portable homes where worms can turn our kitchen scraps into soil that is rich with nitrogen, phosphorous and potassium. They also produce **worm juice** – a liquid that's an excellent fertiliser once it's watered down.

Ask a Big Environmentalist if you can purchase a worm farm, or perhaps you could make your own. Then fill it with kitchen scraps like **tea bags**, **paper towel** and **vegetable scraps** (but no garlic, onion or citrus – worms don't like those).

As long as your farm is in a shady spot and you top it up regularly, you'll have homemade fertiliser in no time!

WATER

We now know that water is one of the ingredients plants need to grow, but how do you know how *much* water your plants need? As well as checking your plant labels, you can use this handy rule of thumb . . . or knuckle!

THE KNUCKLE TEST

Push your finger into the soil around your plant until your first knuckle is underground. If the soil feels dry and your finger comes out clean, your plant is likely ready for some water.

When watering your plants, always remember that plants absorb water through their roots!

There are other tricks you can use to ensure your plants get the right amount of water.

Self-watering pots contain two layers – a tall top layer for your plant and all its soil, and a short bottom layer to catch excess water. This means that your soil won't be waterlogged, and there's always water your plant's roots can stretch to for a drink.

Gradual waterers work very well in outdoor gardens. Recycle an old plastic bottle by asking a Big Environmentalist to create some holes in the lid. Then fill the bottle with water, close it up and poke it into the ground near your plants. Over time, the water will leach into the soil, keeping your plants hydrated!

PROPAGATING PLANTS

Carefully removing part of a plant and helping the offcut grow is called propagating. It's one of the most sustainable ways to expand your garden, because you can use plants you already have! It can also give new life to overcrowded plants.

There are lots of different ways to propagate. You might:

- ◎ take a cutting
- ◎ push part of a long stem into the ground to encourage it to create new roots
- ◎ divide a clumping plant
- ◎ split a bulb
- ◎ or more!

HOW TO TAKE A PLANT CUTTING

1. Ask a Big Environmentalist to cut a small branch or section of stem off your parent plant. Your cutting should be around 15 cm long with a few leaves attached.

2. Carefully pull off the bottom leaves so that the bottom 5-8 cm of your cutting's stem is bare.

3. It's time to pot your cutting! You can place it into a small container of potting mix, but I like to place my cuttings in a jar of water so I can watch the roots grow! Your new plant is ready for soil once its roots are more than 3 cm long.

GARDEN

We've learnt that pollinators like bees and butterflies are an important part of helping plants produce seeds, and that animals and birds are an important part of spreading those seeds.

So we know that wildlife is a **BIG** part of keeping our gardens and our environment healthy.

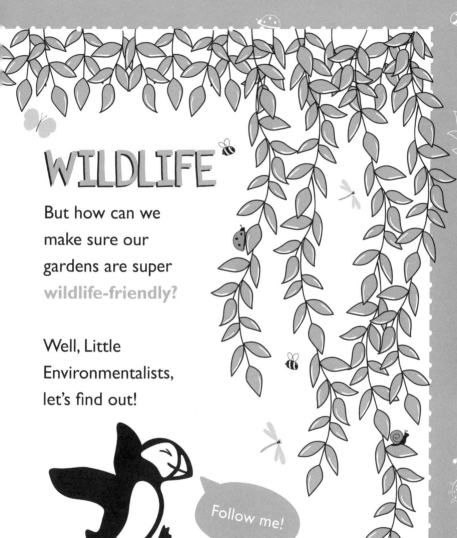

WILDLIFE

But how can we
make sure our
gardens are super
wildlife-friendly?

Well, Little
Environmentalists,
let's find out!

Follow me!

Creatures like birds, frogs, worms, ants, possums, caterpillars and insects are all wildlife. Together with plants, they make up a giant web of living things that all need each other to survive.

But when humans construct buildings and roads, plants are removed and the whole web starts to crumble in a way that affects all living things – including humans.

By returning green space to our backyards and balconies, Little Environmentalists can help provide new habitats for wildlife. We're creating our own LITTLE nature reserves.

It's up to us to protect the environment.

I know we can do it!

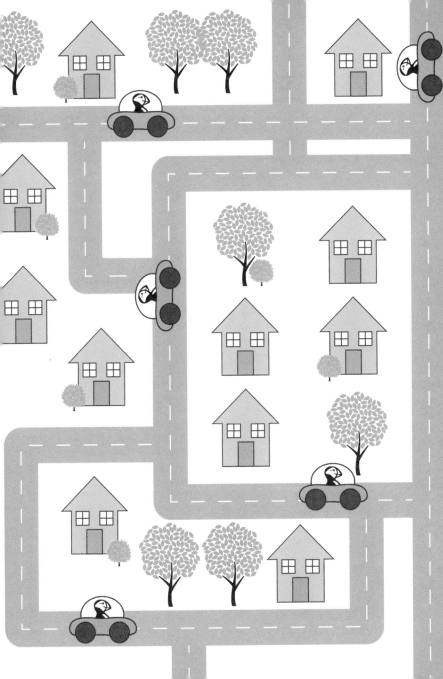

BEE-FRIENDLY GARDENS

Bees aren't just an essential part of keeping our gardens healthy, they're an essential part of keeping the whole planet healthy!

This is because bees are a KEYSTONE SPECIES.

They pollinate most of the food we eat, as well as plants across the entire globe.

KEYSTONE SPECIES

A keystone species is a plant or animal that is crucial to the survival of the environment they live in.

But bee communities are declining. There are fewer and fewer plants for bees to feed from, and lots of the plants we do grow are treated with chemical pesticides and fertilisers that cause bees harm.

Luckily, we can all help!

No matter whether you have a small balcony or a large backyard, you can provide food and shelter to help save the bees.

Let's find out how!

I always try to BEE friendly!

59

Bees don't just pollinate plants. They also carry the pollen and nectar they collect back to their hives. There, they use it to feed their queen and her babies, and to create honey, which keeps bees well-fed when there are no flowers in bloom.

Here are some ways you can make sure your garden is super bee-friendly!

- ◎ Grow lots of flowering plants they can eat.
- ◎ Take care not to use chemical pesticides so their food stays clean.
- ◎ Offer a place to drink by putting out a shallow container of water (or creating shallow areas in a bird bath).

If you have the space, you can also give bees a place to stay by creating a bee hotel.

BEE HOTELS

A bee hotel is a small container that gathers materials bees can form nests in, like bamboo sticks, fennel stems, drilled logs or pipes packed with clay.

Different species of bees look for different things when making their homes, so check which bees are local to your area before placing a hotel.

Hang a bee hotel in a sunny or partially sunny spot between one and two metres off the ground to encourage bees to move into your garden!

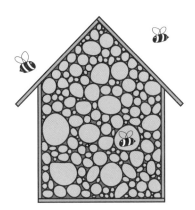

BACKYARD BIRDS

Birds are an important part of any garden. They help pollinate your plants, eat pests and spread seeds. Plus they sing beautifully!

Encouraging birds into your garden is as simple as growing a wide variety of plants, especially ones that are native to your area.

There are other ways to make your garden perfect for birds too, like using only natural pesticides. But no matter how much we'd like to encourage birds into our gardens, there is one thing we Little Environmentalists should not do . . .

. . . we should not feed the birds.

Feeding birds is bad because it steers them away from their natural diet. Human foods like bread or biscuits expand inside a bird's stomach and can mean they won't get hungry in time to eat enough food to survive.

Even giving birds seeds or fruits changes their feeding patterns because it teaches them to rely on us, rather than finding food for themselves.

Having plenty of bird-friendly plants in your garden ensures birds have lots of their usual food available to eat instead!

While we shouldn't leave out birdseed, there is something we *can* add to our gardens to make birds more welcome.

Do you know what it is, Little Environmentalists? It's a bird bath!

A bird bath is a basin filled with around 5 cm of water that provides birds somewhere to drink, bathe and cool down on hot days.

Bird baths should be at least a metre off the ground and away from bushes and structures, so they're tricky for cats and other predators to get to. Putting the basin on a pedestal or hanging it from a tree are excellent options to help keep visiting birds safe.

You can use almost any shallow container to make a bird bath. Why not try an old flat serving bowl?

Once you've assembled your bird bath, add things like pebbles, shells or even marbles under part of the water. This creates shallower zones so insects like bees and butterflies can use the bath too. A stick leaning from the edge of the basin into the water will also help hesitant birds see that their bath is the perfect depth for them to enjoy.

Your garden will be full of birds in no time!

There are lots of other critters that might be part of your garden.

We know worms wriggle through the soil, helping waste like leaf litter break down into the nutrients plants use to grow.

Ladybirds and dragonflies flit from plant to plant, eating insect pests like aphids, mites and scale. Some ladybirds even eat fungus and mildew!

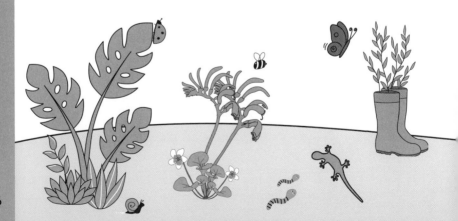

If you have a pond, it could be home to frogs, fish and water insects.

Lizards and skinks love gardens, and can often be seen sunning themselves outside. As well as helping to keep the insect population in balance, they also pollinate flowers!

Butterflies, moths and even bats carry pollen from flower to flower as well.

PLANTING A NATIVE GARDEN

We've learnt some of the ways that gardens help our environment, but do you know what some of the most environmentally friendly gardens are full of?

That's right, it's **native plants!**

This is because native plants are perfectly adapted to grow in their local area.

They often need less water and less fertiliser than non-native plants, they're well-suited to the soil in your backyard and best of all, they help provide the exact homes and food that native wildlife like insects, birds and other animals need.

Are you ready to learn more?

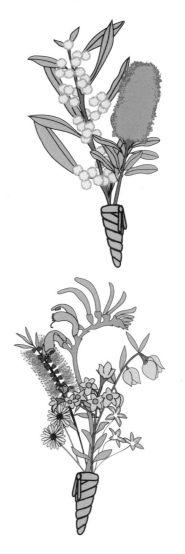

NATIVE PLANTS FOR BACKYARD GARDENS

Fill your garden with plants that are native to your local area and watch your backyard thrive!

Wattle | *Acacia*

Australia's national emblem, with hundreds of different species.

Generally small trees or large shrubs, with fluffy yellow flowers that can appear all year round.

Mint bush | *Prostanthera*

Medium-sized shrubs with purple flowers that emit a soft mint smell.

Each state has different local species.

An excellent plant for attracting bees and butterflies.

Banksia

Can be found in almost every Australian climate.

Varieties ranging from large shrubs to large trees.

Tiny spike-like flowers arranged in clusters that become seed-filled cones.

Lilly Pilly | *Syzygium*

Hedges and trees that flower in summer and produce edible fruit (also called bush cherries) in winter.

An excellent plant for attracting birds, possums and pollinators.

Bottlebrush | *Callistemon*

Extremely hardy trees and shrubs.

Brush-shaped flowers in shades from yellow to red and pink.

Perfect for bringing wildlife to your garden.

NATIVE PLANTS FOR POTS

Some native plants can be tricky to grow in pots, but here are some easier options to get you started!

Australian daisies

Lots of different species, including paper daisies and daisy bushes.

A highly adaptable plant that usually prefers full or part sun.

Flowers come in shades from blue to purple to yellow to red to white and more.

Native violet | *Viola banksii*

A spreading ground cover perfect for hanging pots and thrives Australia-wide.

Native violet has bright green leaves with purple and white flowers that can appear throughout the year.

Native bluebell | *Wahlenbergia stricta*

The floral emblem of the ACT but found over most of Australia.

Very hardy.

Plentiful royal blue flowers that attract bees, butterflies and other pollinators.

Kangaroo paw | *Anigozanthos*

Extremely low-maintenance, but it grows best in full sun.

Tubular, furry flowers in shades of red, orange, yellow, white, green and pink.

Each flower grows on a long stem that can be more than a metre tall.

Boronia

Small shrubs that thrive in part shade and can be found all over Australia.

Bright purple or pink flowers (or one variety has flowers that are velvety brown), shaped like bells or stars.

GROWING A KITCHEN GARDEN

A **kitchen garden** is a garden full of plants you can harvest and eat! Doesn't the thought of growing your own fresh fruits, vegetables and herbs sound wonderful?

LITTLE things like growing some of our own food can have a **BIG** impact on the environment.

This is because one of the best ways we can help our environment is by focusing on being **sustainable**.

There are so many different foods we can grow in a kitchen garden, which means there's something for every kind of garden! No matter what your available space, you can grow your own food.

Here are a few ideas . . .

a vertical wall of leafy greens on your balcony

a raised garden bed in your backyard full of large crops

a **herb garden** on a bright **windowsill**

a collection of **tomato and radish-filled pots** in a sunny spot

fruit vines climbing high on your **fence** or around your **balcony railing**

a **community garden** in your neighbourhood that's got **a little bit of everything**

. . . **or something else entirely!**

ORGANIC GARDENING

Organic gardening uses as few chemicals as possible.

This helps ensure that your plants are growing in a more natural environment.

For a kitchen garden, it means that your harvested fruit, vegetables and herbs are free from artificial fertilisers and pesticides that you don't want to eat!

Artificial chemicals can be very harmful to wildlife too. Growing an organic garden is a **BIG green thumbs up** for the environment.

So how do you fertilise your plants, improve the soil and keep your garden safe from pests if you're not using artificial chemicals?

- ◎ Worm juice is a perfect fertiliser.

- ◎ Compost and worm dirt is excellent at improving your soil.

- ◎ Having lots of different kinds of plants in your garden helps attract an array of wildlife – like birds, spiders, ladybirds and insects – that eat pests.

- ◎ Sticky traps hung from above will catch flying pests, and in-ground traps can stop snails and other bugs before they get to your plants.

Ask your garden centre for even more ideas!

It's important to grow your kitchen garden in the right conditions so that your plants have everything they need for a big harvest.

Edible plants usually need to grow in a space that gets several hours of sunlight a day, and they should be grown in soil with lots of organic matter like compost.

Companion planting means choosing plants that will grow well next to each other.

These can be plants that help ward off pests, attract pollinators or help with the variety in your garden.

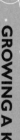

It also means thinking about plants that *don't* grow well together – either because they are targeted by the same pests or because they'll crowd each other out.

A WINDOWSILL HERB GARDEN

A bright, sunny windowsill is the perfect place to start an indoor kitchen garden. And what's one of the plants that packs the most punch in cooking? **Herbs!**

Along with compost-rich soil, you'll need a collection of pots that fit on your windowsill. This is because some herbs, like rosemary, can overtake others, so it's best to plant them separately.

Once your herbs are established, trim them regularly (yum!) and make sure to give them fertiliser during their growing seasons to encourage them to become bushy and full.

If you're feeling very adventurous, try growing your herbs using aquaponics. An aquaponic garden is one where plants grow above a tank full of water . . . and fish!

Tank water is infused with fish poo, which is full of the nutrients plants need. By cycling this water from the tank to the plants and back again, your plants get vital nutrients. The plants then clean the water before it returns to your happy, healthy fish.

We know that growing native plants is one of the most environmentally friendly ways to garden, but did you know that you can include native plants in your kitchen garden too?

LEAFY GREENS

Coastal saltbush, native mint, warrigal greens, native ginger, lemon myrtle and more are excellent additions to salads and add flavour to meals and tea.

EDIBLE FLOWERS

Colour your salads and garnish your meals with edible flowers from native violets, native blueberries or mat rush.

SEEDS AND NUTS
• • • • • • • • •

Harvest native flax or acacia seeds to add as a crunchy salad or yoghurt topper, or grow a macadamia tree and enjoy cracking fresh nuts!

BERRIES
• • • • • • •

Grow muntries, apple-berries, lilly pillies, blue flax lily or pepper berries to eat fresh or make into jam.

FRUIT
• • • • •

Finger lime, Davidson's plum, bush tomato, quandong and more are all delicious native fruits.

GROWING A KITCHEN GARDEN

One of the best ways we can be sustainable in our gardens is by creating new plants out of old plants. There are lots of kitchen scraps that we can use to grow new plants!

GROWING FROM TOPS

When we eat vegetables like carrots, beetroot or turnips, or fruits like pineapple, we don't usually eat the tops.

Instead of composting the tops, give them a little love and turn them into new plants by placing them into a shallow dish of water. When small roots appear, your new plants are ready to be planted into soil!

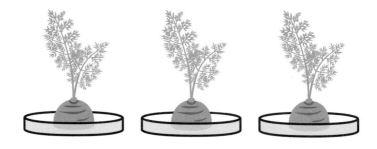

GROWING FROM BOTTOMS

It's not just the tops of fruits and vegetables that can be grown into something new. There are many fruits and vegetables that we usually discard the *bottom* of, like celery, leek, cabbage, bok choy and more.

Place the intact bottoms into a bowl with a few centimetres of water. Leafy greens will begin to regrow almost immediately. Other plants will be ready to be repotted a few days after roots appear.

GROWING FROM SPROUTS

Even though we know it's bad to waste food, sometimes we forget about that potato or bulb of garlic at the back of the pantry, and when we find it again, it has started to grow!

This is perfect for creating even more food. Simply pop your sprouted veg into some soil, keeping the new growth above ground.

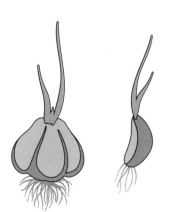

GROWING FROM SEEDS

Next time you eat tomatoes, pumpkin, melons or other seeded fruit and veg, why not save the seeds?

Dry them out on some paper towel and then plant them into seedling mix. With a bit of luck, you'll soon have a whole crop of baby plants to add to your kitchen garden.

Gardens can be as big as a park, or as small as a single pot.

They can also be inside or outside!

Propagating kitchen scraps is a super sustainable way to grow your own food.

Plants recycle carbon dioxide in the air and turn it into oxygen.

Plants make their own food via photosynthesis, using sunlight, carbon dioxide and water.

Plants need nitrogen, phosphorous and potassium to help them grow big and strong.

Flowering plants rely on pollinators like bees, butterflies and birds to be able to produce seeds.

Now it's time to take what we've learnt so far and start gardening!

And remember, the more we learn about gardening, the more we give our environment a **BIG green thumbs up**.

GLOSSARY

CARBON DIOXIDE: a greenhouse gas plants use for photosynthesis.

CHLOROPHYLL: the green pigment in plants that traps and absorbs sunlight.

COMPOST: a mixture of decaying organic matter that is full of nutrients for plants.

GERMINATION: the process in which a seed or spore begins to sprout and starts growing into a plant.

GREENHOUSE GASES: gases in the atmosphere that make the planet too hot.

LEAVES: the parts of a plant that absorb sunlight, usually green, attached to the stem.

PHOTOSYNTHESIS: the process in which plants turn sunlight, water and carbon dioxide into food.

POLLINATION: the process in which pollen is carried between two flowers, allowing seeds to grow.

POLLINATOR: creatures that carry pollen from one flower to another.

PROPAGATION: the process of growing a new plant from part of an existing plant.

ROOTS: the parts of a plant that live underground, anchoring the plant and pulling nutrients and water from the soil.

SEEDS: the parts of a plant that contain embryos that will become new plants.

SPORES: the parts of non-flowering plants that spread and grow into a new plant.

STEM: the spine of a plant, which is full of pathways for nutrients and water to travel.

PUFFIN QUIZ

1. What do plants absorb through their leaves?

2. What kinds of plants use cones and spores to reproduce?

3. What is the process of growing a new plant from part of an existing plant?

4. What animals are likely to use a bird bath?

5. Can you use kitchen scraps to sustainably grow your kitchen garden?

ANSWERS:
1. sunlight 2. non-flowering plants 3. propagating 4. birds, bees and butterflies 5. yes.

A PUFFIN LITTLE BOOK